hen you've been through the fire,
you don't fear the heat—you become it.

BOSS LADY
THE REBIRTH

CHARKIA CAMPBELL

Boss Lady: The Rebirth

By Charkia Campbell

“When you’ve been through the fire,
you don’t fear the heat...
you become it.”

He Loves Curves, Richmond Heights, Ohio

He Loves Curves books may be purchased for educational, business, or sales promotional use. For information, please email charkianeal@yahoo.com

Stacey M. Robinson | Kya Publishing Canada

Cover Design: Chamika Dinesh | Sri Lanka

Page Design: Zeshi | Pakistan

Ebook Design: Osamudiamenabdu Suleiman | Nigeria

Contributions by

ElevatedWaves Publishing Corp. (United States)

ISBN (Paperback): 979-8-9952970-0-0

ISBN (E-book): 979-8-9952970-1-7

Library of Congress Control Number: 2026906747

CONTENT

CONTENT

CHAPTER

Dedication

This book is for women who have cried in silence,

but still got up and faced the world with a smile.

For the one who hid her pain behind strength,

and her tears behind lashes and lip gloss.

For the woman who's been called too much, too big, too loud, or too real,

and still found the courage to love herself anyway.

To the little girl inside me, thank you for holding on

when the world tried to break us.

You taught me how to fight, how to believe, and how to turn every "no" into my next level.

To my family, my husband, and my children: you are my heartbeat,

my push, and my reason for becoming the woman I am today.

You saw light in me when I only saw survival.

And to every Boss Lady, every dreamer, and every woman

finding her way back to herself: this is your reminder that

your story is not over.

You are still becoming.

You are still worthy.

You are still magic.

So here's to the women who rise even when they're tired, who rebuild even when it hurts, and who keep shining because they were born to glow.

Special Dedication

To my amazing best friend, business partner, husband, and big daddy,

Thank you for choosing me, my heart, my journey, and my purpose, and allowing your life to wrap itself around mine so perfectly. You are everything and more than I could ever pray for. There are nights I still whisper to God, "Why do You love me so much to bless me with a man like him?"

You didn't just come to love me, you came to save me.

You saved the woman in me that forgot how to breathe.

You loved the broken parts of me back to life.

You covered me in faith when I couldn't cover myself.

You reminded me what real partnership, real love, and real peace feel like.

You've stood by my side through every storm, even while weathering your own after losing your beautiful mother Nadine, your father Naymon, your grandmother Bernice, and your cousin Rahson Campbell. I saw your strength when your heart was hurting. I saw your faith when life tested every ounce of it. And still, you never stopped covering me.

You are the true MVP, my protector, my peace, and my superhero. The way you carried me through my storms while standing in the middle of your own thunder proves you are truly a son of God.

Thank you for loving me without conditions.

Thank you for seeing me, choosing me, and never letting go even when I didn't have the words. Thank you for believing in my dreams enough to pause your own.

You are my answered prayer, my divine balance, and my forever love.

I love you beyond this moment, beyond this lifetime, and beyond every lifetime after.

Forever your wife,

Charkia Such A Boss 💋

BFQ
PIZZA
BIKE

THE BIRTH OF HE LOVES CURVES

He Loves Curves was born out of my **pain, my healing, and my rediscovery of self-love.**

Before the clothes, before the photoshoots, before the brand, there was me, trying to figure out who I was after my body changed and my confidence broke. I went through many shapes and sizes while fighting lupus, and the world didn't make it any easier. Women who once called me beautiful started calling me fat. I was told to "stop eating," not knowing I was fighting my own silent battle with illness.

I used to look like a Barbie doll, and when the weight came, people used it as a reason to tear me down. I lost myself not just physically, but mentally and emotionally. Depression took over, and I stopped recognizing the woman in the mirror.

But one day, I woke up and decided enough was enough. My size didn't define me, my strength **did**. No matter what people said about me, no matter how I looked, I was going to love myself through it all. I became confident. I became unstoppable. I became me.

When I created **He Loves Curves**, it wasn't just about the curves of my body it was about the curve of my journey. The name came from realizing that through every version of me—

sick, strong, broken, rebuilding—He still loved me. "He" was God, and "Curves" represented every twist and turn of my life that shaped me into the woman I am today.

He Loves Curves stands for more than fashion. It stands for every woman's **smile, confidence, success, story, and self-acceptance.** It's about embracing yourself—every scar, every stretch mark, every curve—and knowing that you are still worthy of love, joy, and confidence.

As I learned to love myself again, I wanted to help other women do the same. Fashion became my ministry, my message, and my healing. It became the way I spoke to other women who were hiding behind pain, judgment, or self-doubt.

So in **2013**, I birthed the vision. And in **2014, He Loves Curves Boutique** officially opened its doors. It wasn't just a store, it was a movement. A safe space where women of all shapes and sizes could walk in and remember that beauty comes in every form.

He Loves Curves

BOSS LADY REFLECTION 💋

You can't heal what you keep hiding.

You can't shine if you keep shrinking.

Every scar tells a story, every curve carries confidence, and every woman has a reason to rise.

He Loves Curves isn't just my brand, it's my reminder that God can turn pain into power, doubt into destiny, and shame into shine.

So wear your story proudly because the world needs your glow.

Personal Reflection:

Becoming the Unstoppable One

See, I was never the "true fashion girl," but I was the ***true believer***. The one who gave herself permission to be unstoppable. I didn't follow trends, I followed faith. And that faith built the woman who refused to quit, who turned vision into victory, and who became *her own definition of style and strength*.

I made a rule that I still stand by today: you couldn't use the word fat in my store, lol. You had to say curves. *I love my curves!* Women would walk in saying, "Girl, I'm fat," and I'd tell them, "You can't buy nothing if you use that word again!" It was never about control; it was about ***redirection.*** About teaching women to speak life over themselves, to love every curve, and to remember that beauty starts with belief.

Take a moment to write your thoughts

BOSS LADY REFLECTION 💋

Being a Boss Lady 💋 isn't about perfection, it's about purpose. It's about showing up, rewriting the rules, and creating spaces where confidence lives. I didn't just sell clothes; I sold self-worth. Every "curve" spoken in that store was a reminder that power begins in how we see ourselves.

So when you walk into any room, hold your head high and remember: **you define the mirror, the mirror doesn't define you.**

Take a moment to write your thoughts

Building a Brand from Scratch

Starting a business sounds cute on paper until you realize it's not just about clothes, logos, or photos. It's about **faith, discipline, and sacrifice.**

When I started He Loves Curves, I didn't have investors, a business plan, or fancy equipment. I had a vision, a name, and a burning desire to make something out of nothing. I didn't even know how deep I was about to go. I just knew I couldn't go back to doubting myself.

I started small. I sold clothes out of my trunk, out of my home, and at pop-up events. I was the buyer, the model, the marketer, the packer, and the delivery driver. There were nights I stayed up tagging clothes until 3 a.m., and mornings I still had to show up like nothing was wrong. Nobody saw the tears, the stress, or the fear. They just saw the pictures and thought, "She got it together."

But the truth was, I was building this brand while rebuilding **me.**

There were times the bills were due, and I had to choose between paying them or restocking inventory. There were moments I wanted to quit because I felt overlooked, underpaid, and undervalued. But every time I thought about giving up, God reminded me that this wasn't just a hustle, this was my purpose.

He Loves Curves became a symbol of **resilience.** It showed that you don't need a perfect plan to start, you just need to start. I didn't wait until I had everything; I worked with what I had and trusted that the rest would come.

I learned how to market through trial and error, how to style photo shoots with nothing but creativity and hustle, and how to make women feel like a million dollars even if their outfit cost forty. I learned that people don't just buy clothes, they buy **confidence.** And that was what I was really selling: the power to feel good in your own skin.

Each setback became a setup for growth. Every "no" taught me how to move smarter.

Every slow day reminded me that consistency wins.

Looking back, I'm proud of the woman who refused to wait for permission. I didn't come from money, I came from **grind** and sometimes that's all you need: a dream big enough to scare you and faith strong enough to sustain you.

BOSS LADY REFLECTION 💋

Don't ever think you need everything to start, all you need is something and a reason why you can't stop.

The best things in life are built from broken places, and the most powerful brands are born from real stories.

So even if you're scared, broke, or tired: show up anyway. Because every seed you plant in faith will one day grow into your legacy.

Personal Reflection:

The Hustle Before the Glow-Up

I'll never forget when I couldn't afford the pretty flyers. So I went to OfficeMax and grabbed the brightest neon papers I could find—green and pink—and wrote He Loves Curves Boutique in big, bold letters. Then I printed out hundreds of them, lol. I was so determined. In my mind, I knew that whenever someone saw that paper, they'd remember the name and recognize who I was: the girl behind He Loves Curves.

Not long after, an old friend helped me find a location she'd heard about. I called the landlord right away, and when he said the rent was $750 for 500 square feet, I laughed and told him, "Here's the truth. I can pay $450 a month and never be late, or I can pay $750 and have you calling me every month asking for the rest." I stood firm on what I could truly afford. I told him if he couldn't do it, I'd just keep hustling out of my trunk. And guess what? God said, Nope, I got you.

The landlord laughed and said, "I like you. I'll take your deal. Just don't be late." And that was it: $450 a month, and it was go time.

I was ready long before my doors opened. I had racks, clothes, and accessories stacked to my ceiling at home. I had never seen this kind of faith in real life, but I believed. I knew one day it would all come together, and when that time came, I wouldn't have to get ready because I stayed ready.

And baby...the work was about to become work.

Take a moment to write your thoughts

BOSS LADY REFLECTION 💋

Building a brand from scratch takes more than money: it takes faith, focus, and fight. I didn't have the luxury of waiting until everything was perfect. I started with what I had, and made it enough.

Every neon flyer, every conversation, every late night taught me this:

- *Consistency is louder than perfection.*
- *Faith is stronger than fear.*
- *And hustle looks good in every color—especially pink and green.*

When you move like you already have it, God aligns the rest.

Take a moment to write your thoughts

The Rise of the Boss Lady 

After building He Loves Curves, I realized I wasn't just building a brand, I was building a voice. A voice for every woman who ever questioned her worth, who hid behind shame, or who forgot how powerful she really was.

Running that boutique taught me more than business. It taught me resilience, faith, and leadership. I learned how to take losses with grace, how to rebuild when doors closed, and how to trust God even when I couldn't trace Him. There were nights I cried on the floor of my store, surrounded by racks of clothes and unanswered prayers, wondering if I was doing enough. But every time I wanted to quit, God whispered, "Keep going."

That's when Boss Lady 💋 was born. Not in success but in surrender. I became the woman who stood on faith when funds were low. The woman who smiled through pain, who built while broken, and who made it her mission to help other women find their light, too.

BOSS LADY REFLECTION 💋

A real Boss Lady 💋 doesn't just build brands, she builds belief.

She doesn't wait for doors to open, she builds her own.

She doesn't chase validation, she *becomes* the proof.

You can lose the store, the job, the relationship, or the plan you had, but never lose your purpose. That's the one thing no one can take from you.

Personal Reflection:

Faith Over Fear

I learned that success is not about how much you sell, it's about how much you serve. Every time a woman walked out of He Loves Curves smiling, I knew I was walking in purpose. That's what kept me going: knowing I was doing Kingdom work through fashion, through words, and through love.

God didn't just give me a boutique. He gave me a ministry. And every woman I dressed was part of my testimony proof that you can start over, glow again, and still win after the storm.

Take a moment to write your thoughts

The Rise of the Boss Lady 

Let's take it back.

I know you've read how I started, what I do, and why, but let me tell you where it really began. I was a 16-year-old mother who was counted out before she even had a chance. Because I was pregnant, my school kicked me out and I had to finish through homeschool. I was removed from my leadership position working with young girls my age all because of my pregnancy.

They told me my life was over. That I'd live in low-income housing forever, raising kids, never paying "real rent," never achieving more than survival.

But what many people didn't know is that I wasn't just a regular 16-year-old pregnant girl. There was a deeper truth behind my story, something I had to carry quietly for a long time: "I was raped."

It was something that was hard for me to speak about, especially to my mother. At that age, I didn't know how to find the words or the strength to tell her (or anyone) everything I had been through. So I held that pain inside and carried it with me.

My mother, not knowing the full truth of what had happened, made a decision out of love. She chose not to risk my life by terminating the pregnancy. At the time, she was simply trying to protect her daughter the best way she knew how.

Looking back now, I can say that it became one of the greatest decisions she could have ever made for me. Because through that moment, God still gave me a gift.

My child.

What others saw as a mistake or the end of my future became one of the greatest blessings of my life. God took a moment that could have broken me and turned it into a purpose that would shape the woman I would become.

But as you've read, God had different plans.

He used what others saw as my ending to become my beginning. I'll tell you the full story in my next book, The Truth to My Untold Story. But until then, keep reading. Because every step from here shows how that young girl turned pain into purpose and became the woman the world now calls Boss Lady 💋.

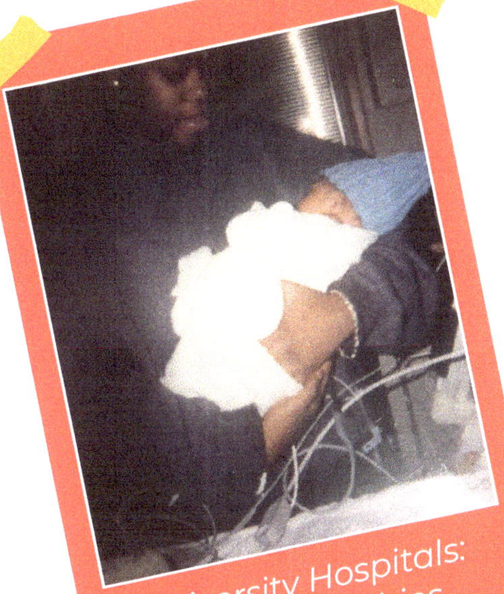

University Hospitals:
Rainbow Babies
Children Hospital

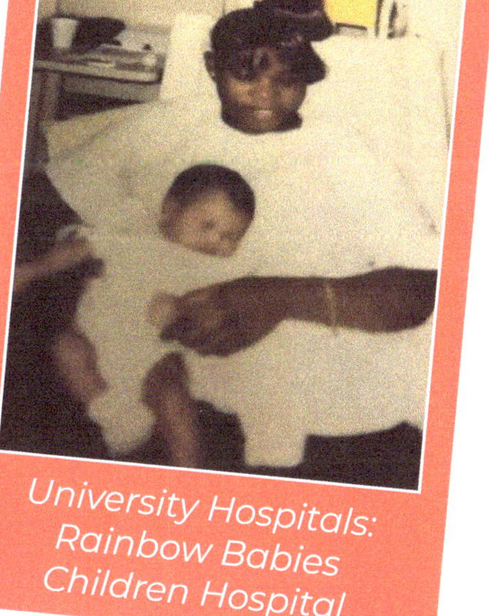

University Hospitals:
Rainbow Babies
Children Hospital

BOSS LADY REFLECTION 💋

Your next chapter doesn't start when things are perfect, it starts when you decide to rise. Keep walking, keep believing, and keep speaking life into every curve of your story.

Because you, Queen, you are the rebirth.

Take a moment to write your thoughts

The Struggles Behind the Success

Everybody loves to clap for the success, but nobody talks about the struggle it takes to get there. They see the photoshoots, the boutique, the fashion shows, and the "Boss Lady" title, but they don't see the nights I cried myself to sleep wondering if I was really built for this.

There were days I wanted to give up. Days when sales were slow, support was silent, and I questioned if I was even walking in my purpose.

People I thought would clap for me started competing with me. Family I thought would stand beside me stopped calling when it wasn't convenient for them to access me. And sometimes, the hardest part wasn't the world, it was my own doubt trying to talk me out of what I knew God told me to do.

I've been betrayed by people I helped, disrespected by people I fed, and overlooked by rooms I was qualified to lead. But every time life tried to break me, God rebuilt me stronger.

I remember sitting in silence one night, completely drained. I said, "Lord, I'm doing everything I can. Why does it feel like I'm losing?" And God reminded me "You're not losing. You're learning."

That hit me deep. Because the truth is, the struggle is part of the success. You can't build strength without pressure. You can't learn loyalty without betrayal. You can't understand peace until you've walked through storms that tried to destroy you.

The struggle made me humble, but it also made me hungry.

It taught me how to protect my energy, how to trust my gut, and how to move in silence until it's time to speak. It made me realize that every time someone counted me out, they were only proving that I didn't need them to win. And through it all, I learned to keep showing up even when I didn't feel like it. Because the Boss Lady in me wasn't built by applause; she was built by adversity.

BOSS LADY REFLECTION 💋

Don't let the pain make you bitter, let it make you better.

Every disappointment is direction. Every struggle is a seed. Every loss is a lesson preparing you for the win.

The ones who laugh at you now will one day have to watch what God does through you. Stay faithful. Stay focused. Stay grounded. Because success isn't about who shines the loudest, it's about who refuses to give up in the dark.

Personal Reflection:

The Faith That Built the Fight

Even when it felt like everything was ending before I had even truly started, my faith almost left me again. The truth is, who doesn't want the ones they love to keep going with them? But at this point, it was bigger than that. I remember sitting for days in a beautiful boutique, surrounded by racks of clothes that no one was coming in to see. Day after day, week after week, month after month. I knew I had to do something different—something that would make me stand out.

One day, I got a call about doing a billboard. The price was way too high, but my mind wouldn't let me dismiss the idea. So, I did my own research. I found the billboard company, called, and spoke with a woman who invited me to come in. We sat and talked for a while, and she gave me advice that changed my entire perspective: "You need to put all your money into advertising for the first three years, because what's the point of having clothes in your store if no one knows who you are?"

That hit me deep.

Of course, I ended up signing the contract for my first billboard, then my second, then my third. Before long, I had over fourteen billboards across the city. That's when the real journey began.

It was a cold season, literally and financially. I was investing so much into advertising that I could barely keep up with buying new inventory. But I reminded myself it's okay. As long as people were learning my name, walking into my store, and seeing my vision come to life, that's all that mattered.

Take a moment to write your thoughts

BOSS LADY REFLECTION

Faith isn't about seeing the way, it's about walking anyway.

When I chose to believe that God was working even in my stillness, everything started to shift. I learned that sometimes He slows the traffic so the right people can see your billboard. So if it feels quiet right now, don't lose faith. The silence is just your setup. Keep investing in you, even when it costs more than you planned, because purpose always pays back with interest.

Take a moment to write your thoughts

The Cost of Greatness—Sacrificing to Receive

People love to talk about the wins the trophies, the sold-out shows, and the success, but nobody wants to talk about the sacrifice it takes to truly receive what you prayed for.

In order to receive, I had to lose.

In order to grow, I had to let go.

And in order to win, I had to first walk through the fire.

He Loves Curves had become one of the most highly ranked boutiques in Cleveland, Ohio, known for its jaw-dropping fashion shows, standing-room-only events, and giving every woman—no matter her shape or size—a chance to own the runway. We sold out shows with over 500 tickets every single time. The lights, the cameras, the interviews, the awards: everything looked perfect on the outside.

But behind the sparkle, darkness was forming quietly. The success was flowing, the profits were rolling, and I thought I had finally made it...until the bottom fell out. I discovered that I had hired a fraudulent accountant who mishandled my finances, left me with income tax liens, unpaid sales taxes, and a trail of financial chaos that nearly destroyed everything I had built.

What hurt the most wasn't just the loss, it was realizing I had trusted the wrong people. I had chosen them, without doing my research, without truly understanding business. That mistake cost me years of hard work, time, and stability.

I lost opportunities, including a major competition I had won but couldn't step forward into, because my financials weren't in order. That was a pain I'll never forget: the kind that humbles you, teaches you, and matures you all at once.

I had to rebuild again, but this time, I did it with self-accountability, not blame. I learned that every downfall is a setup to strengthen your foundation.

While I was trying to hold myself together, my husband was fighting battles of his own. He had just lost both his mother and his father, carrying grief that most people could never imagine, yet he still found the strength to carry me through mine.

When I tell you it was one hell of a roller coaster, I mean it from the soul. Two people grieving, both trying to be strong for each other, and both trying to keep faith alive when everything around us felt like it was falling apart.

Then came the world's biggest shutdown: COVID-19. And even then, my husband didn't let me fall.

When everything stopped, when businesses were forced to close, and when the world was filled with fear, he made sure I was still able to move. He sacrificed his time, his energy, and his own healing, just to make sure I had shipments and boxes coming right to our door.

While the world shut down, my husband kept our vision open.

That was the true test of strength: not money, not fame, but faith and partnership. Even in our darkest moments, love and purpose still showed up. Through every loss, God was preparing me for the kind of wins I could handle—the ones built on wisdom, not ego.

BOSS LADY REFLECTION

Sometimes, your greatest blessings come wrapped in brokenness. The fall doesn't mean failure, it's a lesson dressed in disguise. I lost money, people, and peace... but I found purpose, patience, and power. I learned that true love doesn't just stand beside you, it carries you when you can't walk.

Every storm that tried to drown me only taught me how to swim deeper in faith. So don't curse your struggles, thank them, because what you lose in the process is nothing compared to what God is preparing to replace it with.

Take a moment to write your thoughts

BOSS LADY REFLECTION

"When you've been through the fire, you don't fear the heat—you become it."

The Day Everything Changed

August 28, 2020, four days after my birthday, my life changed forever.

I was working a normal day; the store was filled with customers, laughter in the air. My sister had just dropped my niece off to me, and everything felt light and happy. Then my phone rang from an unfamiliar number.

As always, I answered, "Hello, He Loves Curves, how can I help you?"

It was my son. His voice was in shambles. I could feel his fear through the phone as he cried, "Mommy, please come get me. I was in a very bad car crash. I'm scared, but I'm alive. Please come get me."

My heart raced. I grabbed my niece's hand and told my customers, "I have to go. My son needs me!"

I jumped in my car and started driving toward the scene, trying to make out his words as he gave me directions. He said, "271 South Freeway," and then his phone dropped. All I could hear were loud cries and chaos.

When I arrived, all I saw were flashing lights, twisted metal, and his black car sitting on top of the wall in the middle of the freeway. The driver's door was gone, airbags exploded, glass everywhere. It looked like a bulldozer had crushed it.

I screamed, "Where's my son?!"

The officers said, "The man with the leg injury is on the way to the hospital." They told me he had been hit twice once inside the car and again outside of it and he was bleeding out due to the leg injury.

I drove to the hospital with tears blurring my vision. I wasn't prepared for what the doctors were about to tell me; all I wanted to hear was God's voice say, "He's alive." And He did. My son was alive, but his condition was critical: over forty-five surgeries, two to three surgeries a week, and twenty-five days straight in the hospital with no visits allowed.

Yes, He Loves Curves became my therapy, but I also needed something to stop my mind from racing. I had just opened back up, and my customers needed me. Truthfully, I needed them too. In the process of saving both of them—my son and the business I had birthed—I realized everyone around me had sacrificed something for me to be great. That reminder alone kept me going.

It took me weeks before I even posted on social media, because this wasn't for attention it was real life. My baby boy, my only child, was fighting for his life.

The Hardest Thing a Mother Could Say

I had to face my son, my baby boy, and look him in his eyes to deliver the hardest words I've ever had to say.

"Your life is going to change, and things may be different," I told him, trying to keep my voice from breaking. "But you were picked for this. We're going to have to amputate your left leg to keep you alive. The infection from trying to save it is spreading, and if we don't act now, it could take your life."

I grabbed his hand and said, "I need you to understand this no matter what: there are men with two legs who aren't as powerful as you. We got this."

I remember saying those words to strengthen my own heart just as much as his. I sat beside his bed, holding him tightly until the nurse gently told me my time was up.

When I shut the door behind me, the tears fell faster than I could catch them. In that moment, I felt like I had lied to my son. How could I tell him I understood when I still had both of my legs? I couldn't give him mine. I couldn't trade places with him. As a mother, that feeling was unbearable. In that moment, I felt like I had failed him.

But even through my pain, I thanked God. Because at the end of the day, I would rather buy a leg than a casket. All glory to Him.

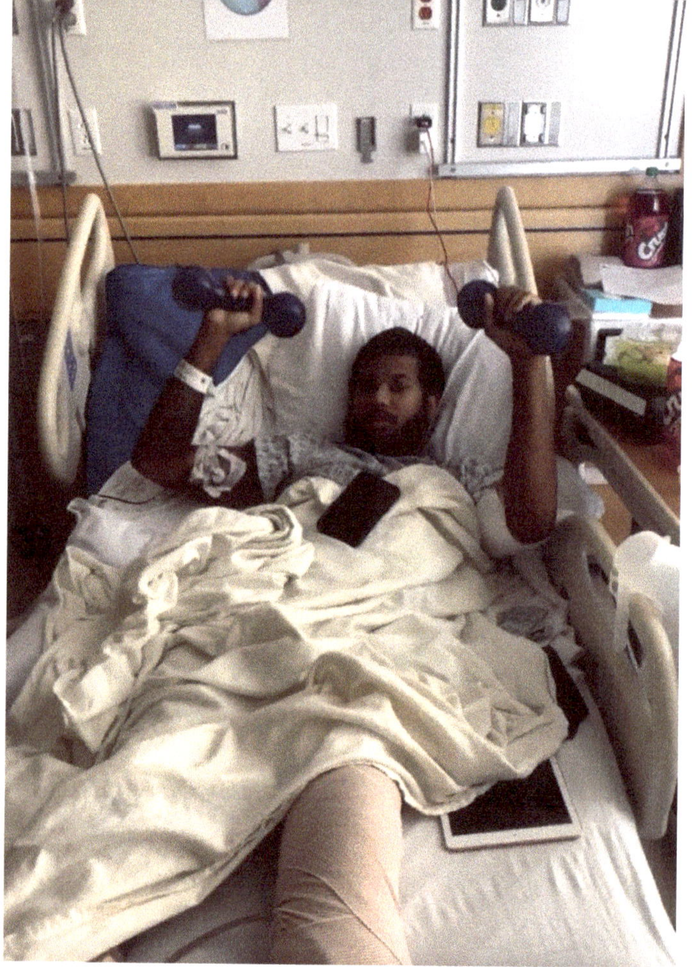

After four long months, I finally received the call that I could bring my son home. But this time, things were different. His left leg had been amputated to save his life. It was a moment that changed everything, yet it was also the moment I realized something powerful. I had given birth to a real superhero.

COVID had tested everything in me—my soul, my patience, my success, and my faith. My son had always been a great athlete, a basketball player, and my best friend. Roy had planted that seed in him when he was just eight years old, and from that moment on, he never gave up on the game he loved.

But now life had given him a new challenge. This time, my son would have to lean on God like never before, because his new beginning would look nothing like his past.

And through it all, the strength of his amazing dad, Chris, stood right beside him. Even when the doctors said he wouldn't be able to walk for another year, his father refused to accept that as the final answer. Chris stood by him every day, working out with him, pushing him to regain his strength, rebuilding his confidence piece by piece.

What doctors believed would take a year, his father helped him accomplish in just three months.

Three months.

Not only was he walking again, but his dad continued training him in the gym week after week, building his strength until he became even more powerful than before. That's when I realized something else: superheroes aren't just born, sometimes they are rebuilt. Through faith, love, family, and the refusal to give up.

BOSS LADY REFLECTION

Sometimes the biggest test of strength isn't rebuilding a business, it's rebuilding your faith when your heart breaks. That moment taught me that even when life knocks the wind out of you, you still have to breathe through it. My son's fight reminded me that God gives His toughest battles to the ones strong enough to stand again.

Through pain, purpose is born, and through loss, love becomes unshakable. I stand again. Through pain, purpose is born, and through loss, love becomes unshakable.

Take a moment to write your thoughts

The Storm Before the Rebirth

They say you never know how strong you are until being strong is the only choice you have left. In my life, that became my reality.

After getting back up, I opened another location and expanded my dream even bigger. I wanted to create a one-stop space where beauty, fashion, and entrepreneurship could live under one roof. The day we cut that ribbon, it felt like I was finally stepping into a new season: healed, focused, and ready to walk fully in my purpose again. But what I didn't know was that another storm was waiting for me.

I remember the day like it was yesterday: October 31, 2022. I got the call that my best friend had passed away. I screamed so loud it felt like my soul left my body. I had never experienced personal loss like that before. I was lost, confused, and numb.

I wasn't prepared for this. My Roy was gone. We had just talked two days before. Roy had been there from the start with my son, and was with me when I first opened my boutique. When I mentioned the vision, he said, "Let's go. What do you need me to do?"

He was one of my biggest supporters, sending people from everywhere, advertising me like crazy, holding down every fashion show, and standing beside my husband at our wedding. He wasn't just my friend; he was my family, my heart. Roy was that one true friend who gave it to me straight and believed in my dream like it was his own.

He was a part of my "He Loves Curves," and part of why it stood strong.

My Big Brother, Chuckie

Then came December 31, 2022.

Chuckie was the big brother by birth, but I always acted like the big sister. I was the one running all my siblings! He helped me so much at my first boutique location, keeping my back room organized, fixing things, and doing whatever I needed without hesitation. He always had my back. There was nothing I couldn't ask of him. He was my big brother in every way that mattered.

When he saw my new location, he smiled and said, "Okay, sis, I see you doing your Oprah thing!"

I laughed so hard! I was so excited he came to see me. That moment meant everything.

I had kissed and hugged my big brother at my new location, proudly introducing him to everyone there. Hours later, my phone rang again, this time telling me he was gone. He had been murdered, his life taken by a man who broke into his apartment. I remember collapsing to the floor, racing to him, only to face the truth no sister should ever have to see: the only big brother I had—the one I had just said "I love you" to—was gone.

I couldn't breathe. I couldn't understand. I was angry, broken, and completely empty. I was mad.

And then came another heartbreak on May 22, 2023. This one came completely out of the blue. I'll keep it short: it went from my brother dropping hot water on his foot, to refusing to go to the doctor, to finally going in on a Wednesday... maybe needing surgery on Thursday... and on Friday, he was asleep and bleeding from the brain. By Saturday, they called me to make the hardest decision of my life, to 'pull the plug' on one of my baby brothers.

He wasn't blood, but he was mine. My god-brother. My heart.

I remember saying, "This is impossible." It felt like I was living outside my own body like life was moving, but I wasn't in it. This was the same person I had just sat on the bed with, laughing, and talking about me getting ready to accept an award. I raised him since he was 18.

I'll never forget that moment. He looked at me and said, "Hug me tight, sis."

I laughed and said, "I'm not hugging you too tight, boy. The last brother I hugged left me."

Then I said, "I'll see you later," and gave him a high-five. "I love you, kiddo."

I think you can guess the rest... he left me too.

EXIT

When the Light Faded

Just when I thought the pain couldn't get any heavier, December 5, 2023 came.

My mother's mom (my grandmother), my light, my teacher, my biggest supporter, my number one fan, took her last breath. She was my foundation. The one who taught me how to hustle, how to pray, and how to stand tall no matter what life threw at me.

She was the voice that reminded me, "Baby, keep your head up and don't ever let them see you break." She gave me the kind of love that shaped who I am: firm, faithful, and fearless.

Losing her felt like losing my compass. The world got quieter, but even in her absence, I still hear her in my spirit, pushing me to keep going, to stay strong, and to finish what she helped me start.

Her lessons didn't die with her: they live in me. Every move I make, every door I open, every win I celebrate... that's her legacy continuing through me.

Before I could even process that loss, on December 16, 2023, my father's dad (my grandfather) passed away. It felt like my heart was losing every piece that helped it beat. He was the protector of our family—quiet but strong; firm but loving. Losing him right after losing my grandmother felt unreal, and like grief wouldn't give me a moment to breathe.

Even through the pain, I felt God whisper, "This isn't the end, it's the passing of the torch." Their love, their faith, their strength: it all lives in me now. I carry them with every step I take, every dream I chase, and every storm I survive.

BOSS LADY REFLECTION

Sometimes, God has to break your heart to rebuild your strength.

You can't skip the pain if you want the power.

The losses nearly destroyed me, but they also purified me. They taught me that grief can grow you, and pain can position you. So when life feels like it's falling apart, remember this:

you're not being buried you're being planted. And when you rise again, you'll bloom with purpose.

Take a moment to write your thoughts

The Rebirth Begins

After losing so much, I reached a place where silence became my teacher and faith became my only strength. I didn't know how to keep standing, but somehow, I did. Piece by piece, God started rebuilding me—not into who I was, but into who I was meant to be.

Those losses broke me wide open, but they also made room for a new version of me to rise stronger, wiser, softer, and more intentional. It was in that season of pain that Boss Lady: The Rebirth was born. Not out of perfection, but out of perseverance. Not because I had it all together, but because I refused to stay broken.

The Birth of Vendetta's Box—Rebuilding from the Ashes

After all the losses, heartbreaks, and silent nights, I didn't think I had anything left in me to build again.

My spirit was tired.

My heart was heavy.

My body was present, but my mind was still somewhere between grief and survival.

When God gives you a purpose, He won't let you stay broken for too long. He'll shake you, test you, and then whisper, "Now rise." When that whisper came, I wasn't alone.

My husband, my King, my protector, and my peace became my strength when I had none left. Even through his own pain, after losing both his parents, he still carried me through mine. He prayed over me when I couldn't pray for myself. He reminded me that the woman God created me to be was still in there. She was just tired, not gone.

There were nights he'd just sit beside me in silence because he knew words couldn't fix what my heart was feeling. That's real love: when someone stands with you through the storms you can't even explain.

My family also became my anchor. They showed up, held me, checked on me, and refused to let me fade into depression. My children gave me purpose again: their smiles reminded me that life wasn't done giving. They still needed their mom to be that strong woman I'd always taught them to be proud of.

Slowly, piece by piece, I began to find myself again.

It wasn't overnight. It took prayer, patience, and a lot of grace. I started to remember who I was and more importantly, why I started.

One morning, I woke up, looked in the mirror, and said out loud, "I'm not done." That's the moment I decided to rebuild. Not from where I left off, but from a new place. A stronger place. The old me was gone... but the new me was ready.

That's when Vendetta's Box was born: not out of business plans or perfect timing, but out of faith, family, and fire.

Vendetta's Box is the ultimate turn-key empire where we provide a fully operational, brick-and-mortar storefront designed for the entrepreneur who refuses to choose between their career and their calling. They can keep their 9-5 security while our professional management team handles the daily grind. It's their business, their brand, and their building—minus the overhead of their presence.

The Highs and Lows of Building Again

When I started Vendetta's Box, I didn't just want a business, I wanted a movement. A space where other entrepreneurs could walk in and feel seen, supported, and safe. I wanted to create a place that gave people opportunity without judgment or limits, but here's the truth no one prepares you for: when you start building again, you also start attracting every kind of energy ...the good, the bad, and the lessons in between.

Some people came to grow with me. Others came to use me. A few came just to see if I'd fail again. I learned quickly that everyone who smiles in your face isn't standing in your corner. There's a difference between friendships and business-ships, and when you mix the two without boundaries, it can cost you peace, time, and focus.

I used to think loyalty meant doing everything for everybody, until I realized loyalty without limits leads to burnout. I had to learn that everyone can't sit at your table just because you built it.

The highs of building were beautiful: watching others win, seeing ideas turn into income, and knowing I was part of something bigger than myself. The lows were real too: disappointment, broken trust, and learning that some people loved my light...until it started shining brighter than theirs.

Still, through every up and down, I chose to keep my heart pure and my mission solid because I knew that Vendetta's Box wasn't just mine, it was God's assignment. When something is purpose-driven, no person can block what God has already promised.

BOSS LADY REFLECTION 💋

Rebuilding doesn't mean returning, it means rising wiser. God will strip you, shake you, and shift you until your circle matches your calling.

Not everyone who claps for you is for you, and not every loss is meant to be replaced. Some are meant to be remembered.

The true test isn't how many times you fall, it's how many times you rise and still love out loud because the woman who's been through the fire doesn't just rebuild—she becomes the fire.

Take a moment to write your thoughts

Boss Lady Mindset 💋

Becoming a Boss Lady isn't just about the business, it's also about the mindset. You can have all the money, all the followers, and all the recognition in the world, but if your spirit isn't in alignment, you'll still feel empty inside.

After everything I had been through: the pain, the loss, the betrayal, and the rebuilding, I had to sit still and relearn who I was.

Not the businesswoman.

Not the mother.

Not the wife.

But the woman God called me to be.

I had to redefine success, because success isn't just a storefront, a car, or a title: it's peace. It's waking up and choosing not to break. It's learning to let go without losing love, and it's standing tall when life tries to fold you.

I learned that peace costs something and baby, it's not cheap!

It costs boundaries.

It costs saying "no" when your heart wants to say "yes."

It costs walking away from people you once prayed for.

It costs silence when your ego wants to clap back.

The Boss Lady Mindset is knowing when to pause, when to pray, and when to pivot. It's understanding that every closed door isn't rejection it's redirection. I stopped chasing validation and started chasing alignment. I stopped asking, "Why me?" and started saying, "Thank you, God, for choosing me." Once you realize you're chosen, you stop questioning the challenges, and you start understanding the purpose behind them.

The Inner Work

The Inner Work

Boss Lady energy isn't built overnight, it's grown in seasons of discomfort, silence, and surrender.

There were days I had to talk to myself like I was my own best friend. Days where I'd look in the mirror and remind myself: "You've been through worse, and you're still standing."

I started journaling, praying more, and protecting my peace like it was my last breath. I learned that healing doesn't mean you forget, it means that you stop letting the pain control you.

The more I healed, the more clearly I saw my path. I realized I didn't need to compete I needed to create.

I didn't need to prove I needed to produce.

I didn't need to fit in because I was born to stand out.

BOSS LADY REFLECTION

Being a Boss Lady isn't about power, it's about purpose. It's not about being the loudest in the room, it's about being the most intentional. Real Bosses don't just build businesses, they build people, peace, and legacies.

Fix your crown, protect your energy, and walk boldly in who God designed you to be! Once you master your mindset, you can conquer anything.

Take a moment to write your thoughts

It's Only the Beginning

As I look back over every chapter of my life—the highs, the heartbreaks, the tears, and the triumphs—I can honestly say every single part was necessary.

Every loss taught me gratitude.

Every betrayal taught me boundaries.

Every delay taught me discipline.

Every comeback taught me who I truly am.

I used to think success was about proving people wrong, but now I know it's about proving God right. Every time I thought it was over, He showed me it was only a new beginning.

Every time I felt empty, He poured something greater inside me. From He Loves Curves to Vendetta's Box, from pain to purpose, from silence to spotlight, I found me again. Not the same me, but the better me. The healed, wise, grounded, and grateful woman who understands that everything she went through was preparation for the next level.

I've learned that your story never really ends, it just transforms, and sometimes the things that tried to break you were really just building you.

To every woman reading this—the dreamer, the builder, the fighter, the survivor—remember this: you are the blueprint. You are the shift. You are the testimony that others need to see.

This isn't goodbye it's to be continued, because the story of Boss Lady Charkia Campbell is still being written... and trust me, the best chapters are still ahead.

BOSS LADY REFLECTION

Never apologize for evolving.

Never dim your light to make others comfortable.

Never forget every storm you survive comes with a rainbow that has your name on it.

You've read the story. You've felt the pain. You've seen the growth. This is just the first book, the first testimony. Just like this book was written in one night, the story is still being written...and it's only getting better.

HE LOVES Curves BOUTIQUE

Take a moment to write your thoughts

Acknowledge-ments

Thank You to the World's Strongest Mother

Mommy,

Thank you for my gifts.

Thank you for my power.

Thank you for my confidence.

Thank you for using your life to raise me to teach me how to stand tall, love hard, and never settle.

I'll never forget when I was sixteen, scared and unsure, and you looked me in my eyes and said, "Your life doesn't have to stop because of a baby. He's our baby. Your life doesn't change, it gets greater. Now go work for it. Show the world who you are."

Those words became the foundation of my strength. You didn't just raise a daughter, you raised a woman who learned how to turn pain into power and faith into fuel.

Thank you, Mommy, for showing me what real strength looks like. Everything I am and everything I've become, carries your heartbeat.

Thank You to My Daddy

I'm such a Daddy's girl.

You gave me my hustle, taught me how to navigate through any endeavor, and gave me a heart that knows no fear. Your lessons taught me to face the world head-on bold, brave, and unshakable.

To My Big Sister, Zakia

Thank you for carrying my emotions when mine felt too heavy to hold. When I couldn't cry, you cried for me. When I felt weak, you felt for me. They call you the heart and me the brain. But truthfully, you've always been a part of both in me. Your love has been my safe place, my softness, my understanding.

To My Little Sister, Stacey

Thank you for being my strength when I couldn't find my own. You always called me right on time. In moments when I was feeling down on myself without showing it or even saying a word. Somehow, you just knew. When I didn't believe in myself, you reminded me who I was. You made me feel like I was the world's best even on my worst days.

Watching you grow into your power has been nothing short of inspiring. You are the muscle, the push and the fire that keeps me going.

To My Baby Brother, Romeo

Thank you for showing me it's okay to live life our own way; unapologetically and free. You are the clouds to me reminding me to move, to shift, to breathe, and to let life flow the way it was meant to.Your spirit is a reminder that freedom is a choice, and you stand in yours boldly.

In Loving Memory of My Big Brother, Chuckie

RIP, we love you forever. Your presence still lives in us.

To My God Brother, Shawn

RIP, I love you. You will always be a part of me.

Author's Note

When I started this journey, I didn't plan on writing a book, I was just living my truth, and trying to survive what was meant to destroy me. As I grew, I realized my story wasn't just for me...it was for every woman who's ever had to rebuild herself from broken pieces.

He Loves Curves was my success.

Vendetta's Box became my healing.

This book is my rebirth, a mirror for every woman who's ever lost herself trying to please the world, and then found her power when she finally chose herself. I've had to fight through sickness, judgment, heartbreak, and doubt, but I also learned that grace is stronger than pain, and faith can rebuild anything.

I turned every "why me?" into "watch me."

My hope is that as you read these pages, you see yourself somewhere between the lines—not just in the struggle, but also in the comeback. I want you to remember that your story matters, your journey is sacred, and that your voice deserves to be heard.

To every reader, sister, dreamer, and boss who's ever questioned her worth: walk in your power, wear your story proudly, and never shrink for anyone. The moment you realize you were chosen not just to survive, but to shine, that's when everything changes.

With love and purpose,

~ Charkia Such A Boss

The Voice That Kept Me

"The world saw the Boss Lady.
But the man who loved her
watched the woman fight her way back to life."

Through His Eyes

The hardest thing I ever had to do... was watch my wife endure the pain of our son.

My wife was at the top of her career. All the grinding, all the long nights, and all of the consistent days at the store had finally paid off. I watched her build something from nothing with her own hands. I watched her sacrifice sleep, comfort, and peace just to chase a vision that lived inside her heart; and it was finally working.

Then one moment changed everything. The car crash.

The call that could have taken our son from us forever. I will never forget the look in her eyes that day. It was the first time in my life that I saw my wife truly break. Not the kind of broken where someone cries and moves on. This was deeper. This was a mother watching the life she carried, the child she nurtured, the boy she raised, fighting to survive. And in that moment, I knew something, I could not fall apart. Not then. Not when my family needed me the most.

The truth is, I was already carrying my own grief. I had lost my father, my mother, my grandmother, and my cousin. Those wounds were still fresh. Those losses were still heavy on my heart. But as a man, as her husband, as the father of our son – My pain had to wait. So I put it on pause.

While she was trying to hold herself together as a mother, I had to hold the foundation of our family. I had to be strong enough to help save our son and strong enough to help heal my wife.

That wasn't easy. Some nights I prayed harder than I ever had before. Some nights I sat in silence asking God to give me strength I didn't even know I had. But I trusted something bigger than me. I trusted that God had us and I trusted that I had them.

When it came to her business, I refused to let everything she built disappear. Not even COVID could stop me from working. No matter what the world looked like around us, I was going to make sure she didn't lose a beat. Because I knew the business wasn't just a business. It was her dream.

Even with all the love, all the effort, and all the strength, my wife was still broken, and as her husband, that was one of the hardest things I had to accept. I wanted to fix it, I wanted to take the pain away; but some battles you can't fight for someone. They have to walk through the fire themselves. So I did the only thing I could do. I covered her.

Between me and God, I made a promise that no matter how long it took, I would protect her while she found herself again. Months, Years, However long it took.

But through all the pain, it wasn't all bad.

One of the most special moments of this journey came during one of my wife's fashion shows. Our son had always walked in her shows. It was something special between them. Something that made her proud every single time. But after the accident, the doctors told us something that crushed her. They said our son wouldn't walk for a year.

For my wife, that wasn't an option. I remember her looking at me like she already knew the outcome. She said, "The show is in three months and he will walk. I know you can do it."

When I tell you the pressure was on me, the pressure was on me. Three days after our son came home from the hospital, I fired the hospital therapist. I became his trainer.

EMPIRE

Day after day I worked with him. Through the pain, through the frustration, through the doubt. Some days were hard. Some days I questioned if we were pushing too much.

But my son believed in me and my wife never doubted for a second. With the help of God, the strength of my son, and the faith of my wife pushing me every single day, our son took his first steps on March 21, 2021. 3 months after the doctors said it would take a year.I DID IT! At that moment I saw something in my wife's eyes again, not the brokenness, but the fire. The same fire that made her the Boss Lady in the first place.

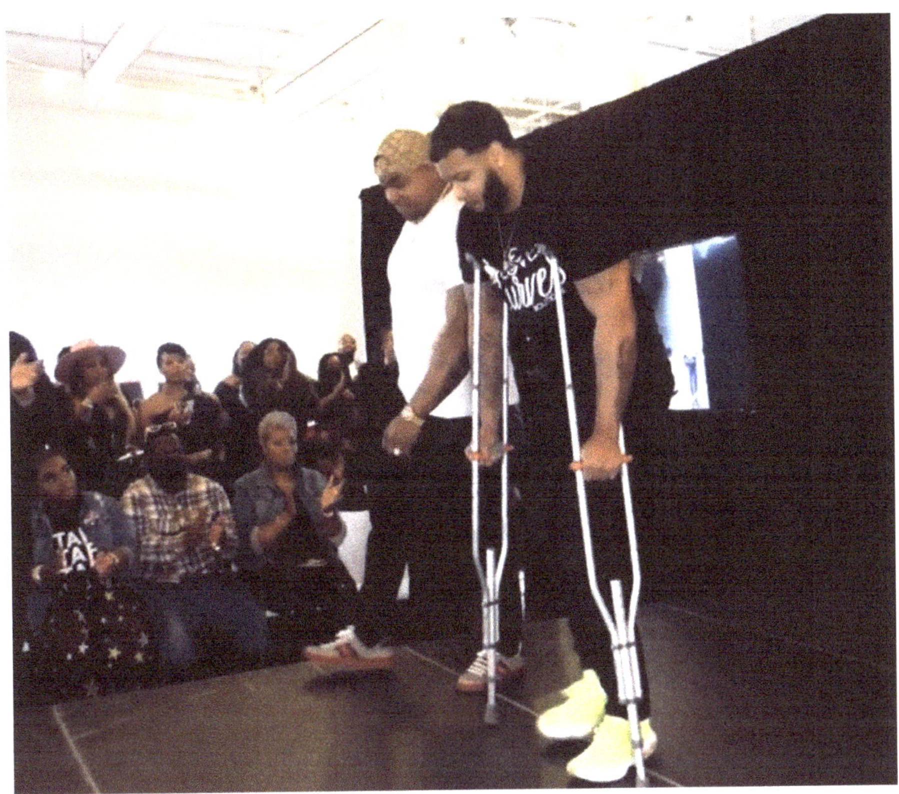

There was another moment I will never forget. One night my wife looked at me with tears in her eyes and asked a question that I knew came from the deepest part of her soul. She said, "What do I do now? I feel lost." And I told her something I truly believed. I said, "Become Charkia again. Not the Boss Lady, not the woman the world sees. Become the woman who had the dream in the beginning, the woman who was hungry, the woman who was motivated when nobody believed yet. Start there and build again." Sometimes the strongest thing you can do in life is go back and find the person you were before the world tried to break you.

What most people don't see is the part of our life that stays behind closed doors. My wife lives with lupus. That's a fight the outside world doesn't see. So every night I stay awake a little longer. I never go to sleep before she does. I watch her breathe, I make sure she doesn't have a seizure in her sleep, I make sure she wakes up. Loving her means protecting her in ways people will never understand.

The world sees the Boss Lady; they see the strength, the success and the confidence. But I see the warrior behind the title, the woman who fought through grief, the woman who carried pain and still kept going, the woman who fell apart and who found the strength to rise again.

And after everything we've been through, She's still my peace.

If you ask me the truth about the rebirth of the Boss Lady, it didn't happen on a stage and it didn't happen inside her business. I watched it happen slowly, piece by piece inside our home; In the tears she cried when nobody was watching, in the prayers she whispered when she thought God wasn't answering, in the days she wanted to give up but chose to stand back up anyway. That's where the rebirth really happened and that's why I know something most people don't.

The Boss Lady they see today, she didn't just rise, she survived the fire that was meant to destroy her and if God asked me again to carry her through that storm, I would do it every single time because loving her was never a burden, It was an honor.

Signed,

Her Husband, Mr. Campbell

About the Author

Charkia Campbell is a visionary entrepreneur, motivational speaker, and community leader from Cleveland, Ohio. Known for turning pain into purpose, she has built multiple successful brands including He Loves Curves Boutique and Vendetta's Box Smart Boutique, a one-of-a kind retail experience that empowers entrepreneurs to scale from online to brick-and-mortar ownership.

Charkia's journey hasn't been easy, it's been real.

From battling illness and loss to rebuilding her businesses and faith, she's proven that no matter how many times life knocks you down, you can rise again stronger, wiser, and more unstoppable than ever.

A proud wife, mother, mentor, and advocate for youth empowerment, Charkia uses her platforms to inspire others to heal, grow, and build legacies that last. Her mission is simple: to teach others that your story is your power, and your come back will always speak louder than your setbacks.

Through her upcoming Part 2 eBook, mentorship programs, and Vendetta's Box Academy, she continues to pour into others helping dreamers become Bosses.

"I don't just build businesses, I build people."

Forever Isnt Long Enough

www.ingramcontent.com/pod-product-compliance
Ingram Content Group UK Ltd.
Pitfield, Milton Keynes, MK11 3LW, UK
UKHW062301290726
14090UKWH00017B/827